BLACKBERRY
MOLASSES

BLACKBERRY MOLASSES

A play in five parts

INSPIRATION
Poetry and lyrics

BY

JOVIAL SMITH

iUniverse, Inc.
Bloomington

Blackberry Molasses

iUniverse books may be ordered through booksellers or by contacting:

iUniverse
1663 Liberty Drive
Bloomington, IN 47403
www.iuniverse.com
1-800-Authors (1-800-288-4677)

ISBN: 978-1-4697-8148-8 (sc)
ISBN: 978-1-4697-8150-1 (hc)
ISBN: 978-1-4697-8149-5 (ebk)

Printed in the United States of America

iUniverse rev. date: 04/19/2012

CONTENTS

Preface...ix
Introduction....................................xi
Cast of Characters.............................xiii
Setting..xvii

ACTS ONE—ACT FIVE

ACT I
ACT ONE SCENE ONE Front Yard Summer 2007....3
ACT ONE SCENE TWO A living room.............7
ACT ONE SCENE THREE Desera's Bedroom.......11
ACT ONE SCENE FOUR Julie's front patio.....15
ACT ONE SCENE FIVE Melanie's office........19
ACT ONE SCENE SIX Brandon's restaurant
   "Eddie Lee's Soul food." 23
ACT ONE SCENE SEVEN Stefanie's Apartment...27
ACT ONE SCENE EIGHT Ebony and Traci's
   Bedroom. 31

ACT II
ACT TWO SCENE ONE Desera's office July
   2008-Summer. 35
ACT TWO SCENE TWO Janelle's beauty shop
   "New Beginnings." 39
ACT TWO SCENE THREE "The Olympia Café......43

ACT TWO SCENE FOUR Janelle's Apartment.....47
ACT TWO SCENE FIVE Desera's apartment......51
ACT TWO SCENE SIX: Desera's apartment.
   "The Olympia Café'." 55
ACT TWO SCENE SEVEN (Professional
   Performing Arts School) 61

ACT III
ACT THREE SCENE ONE(Annual Christmas
   Party. December 2008) 65
ACT TRREE SCENE TWO "The New York Star"
   Headquarters January 2009. 69
ACT THREE SCENE THREE "The restaurant
   "Epiphany's." 71
ACT THREE SCENE FOUR Janelle's apartment
   Mid January 2009. 75
ACT THREE SCENE FIVE The "New York Star"...79
ACT THREE SCENE SIX Central Park April
   2009. 83
ACT THREE SCENE SEVEN Janelle's patio
   May 2009. 87

ACT IV
ACT FOUR SCENE ONE Derek's apartment.......91
ACT FOUR SCENE TWO Anthony's Visit April
   2010. 95
ACT FOUR SCENE THREE The Restaurant
   "Epiphany's" May 2010. 99
ACT FOUR SCENE FOUR Janelle's wedding.
   Summer 2010. 103
ACT FOUR SCENE FIVE Derek's and Desera's
   engagement party Fall 2010. 109

ACT V

ACT FIVE SCENE ONE "The New York Star"
   Headquarters." 113

About the Author........................117

Preface

The play "Blackberry Molasses" is an inspirational story about a young woman who finds her voice through her writing. This play is written to encourage and inspire readers to pursue their dreams. This particular storyline was created with the intent to catch the audience's attention. Many readers' will be able to relate to one or more characters and the adversities which they endured. From the beginning of *Blackberry Molasses*" to the Epilogue, one will see the significance of strength and perseverance illustrated through the Maple and Blackberry Trees. The main character Desera finds strength and perseverance through her writing. Desera is one of the main characters that will hopefully draw your attention and causes you to reflect on our life. After reading *Blackberry Molasses*" I *hope the audience will not only learn something from it, but will apply the various positive messages to his or her lives.*

In my final Act I choose Eric Benet and Tamie rendition of *Spend My Life with You." This song seemed very appropriate for a wedding because of the beautiful lyrics . . .*

DEDICATION: *I would like to give a special thanks to my second cousin Joan Singleton for assisting me through the Editorial process. (Jovial Smith)*

Introduction
The Play "Blackberry Molasses"

"Blackberry Molasses" is about a 27 young African American woman named Desera Harrison who lives in Atlanta Georgia with her mother Janelle and her 14 year old twin sisters Ebony and Traci. Desera desires to be a freelance writer. As she discovers her gift of writing, Desera comes across her father Anthony who's now a recovery alcoholic. She finds peace and serenity through her writing. After writing non-stop for weeks, Desera decides to send her writings to *The New York Star.*" When she finally hears back from *The New York Star,*" Representative Melanie Williams, Desera is elated that this company is willing to let her write her inspirational story about her life that will surely help people who are faced with the same adversities as she once had.

Blackberry Molasses is a play that symbolizes strength and perseverance. In this play, the Blackberry and Maple trees represent a sweet fragrance that feels the atmosphere. The trees symbolizes strength and perseverance that Desera and her family goes through in-order to prosper. Strength is an important element in this remarkable play because it illustrates Desera Harrison and her family's decision to leave their past behind and peruse their dreams. Strength is also a vital element in *"Blackberry Molasses" because* of Desera's ability to leave her hometown, Atlanta, Georgia to move to New York City. Perseverance is illustrated throughout the play through Desera's pursuing her dream of becoming a freelance writer for one of the largest newspaper publications in New York, *"The New York Star."* Despite the many disappointments and heartaches that Desera and her family have endured, Desera accomplishes her dream of becoming a Journal Analyst.

Jovial (Joy) Smith

Cast of Characters

Desera—An inspiring Freelance writer who shares her story of how she didn't allow her situation with her father to determine the outcome of her life.

Janelle—She's the mother of Desera, Ebony, and Traci. She owns her own beauty shop called *"New Beginnings" which symbolizes* her family starting over and leaving their past behind.

Anthony—He's the father of Desera, Ebony, and Traci. He's a recovering alcoholic. Anthony has stage three Prostate cancer and isn't expected to live much longer.

Ebony—She is Traci's twin sister and Desera's younger sister. She has a remarkable gift of writing.

Traci—She has an amazing gift of painting and she's Desera's younger sister.

Melanie Williams—a representative from *"The New York Star"*, who discovers Desera's writings and gives her the opportunity to become a freelance writer that helps others, overcome their situation.

Derek—He is the Journalist at *"The New York Star." His friend introduces him to Desera and eventually becomes Desera's fiancé`.*

Brandon—Desera's best friend from Atlanta Georgia.

Lisa—Desera's long time friend failed to meet her at *"The Olympia Cafe."*

Staci-She is a Journal Analyst that introduces Derek to Desera at an annual Christmas party.

Julie-Desera's childhood friend, who encourages her to write.

Kevin-Janelle's current husband who she meets in New York. He loves her unconditionally and is very supportive.

Stefanie-Desera's best friend from Atlanta Georgia.

Regina—A young woman who is a victim of physical abuse and finds closer by reading Desera's story.

Roger-Evette's husband, Janelle's father and Desera, Ebony, and Traci's Grandfather from Atlanta Georgia.

Evette-Roger's wife, Janelle's mother and Desera, Ebony, and Traci's Grandmother from Atlanta Georgia.

Setting

This is a light brown two story brick house in the country. The scenery is beautiful and refreshing. The breeze from the calm wind is cool and calming. There are Black Berry and Maple tress surrounding the house that gives off a sweet fragrance throughout the atmosphere. In the front, there is a silver gate that stretches about six feet high and six feet long. Inside the silver gate, there's a horse shoe driveway, surrounded by a beautiful rose garden and a stone female angel waterfall. There's a beautiful pond in the backyard filled with multi-colored pebbles.

BLACKBERRY MOLASSES

ACTS ONE—ACT FIVE

AT RISE:

ACT ONE SCENE ONE Front Yard Summer 2007.

    (Somewhere in Atlanta Georgia in the front yard of their light brown two storied house. Desera and her two younger twin sisters Traci and Ebony are lying on their Grandmother's multicolored quilt.)

(The sun is shining down on Desera, Traci, and Ebony. The calm breeze gently passes through the green grass and then sweeps through each of the girl's hair.)

(Desera glances over at Traci and Ebony and smiles.)

        DESERA
Traci and Ebony, what are you two doing?

        TRACI
Enjoying the fresh air. Looking at all of the beautiful trees.

        EBONY
Oh, I am looking up at the Maple and Blackberry trees. Wow, they are tall and shinning.

(As they are lying on their Grandmother's quilt, they are captivated by the beautiful scenery.)

3

                    DESERA
The sound of the cool wind is like a sweet melody
in our ears. The tall Maple and Blackberry
tress surrounding us, give off a very sweet
fragrance.

(Desera rolls over on her left side and glances
at Ebony and Traci.)

                    EBONY
Hey Desera, you see the tall Berry tree straight
ahead.

                    DESERA (Lifts her head.)
Yes, I see.

                    EBONY
I wonder how long did it take this Berry tree
to grow?

                    DESERA
I don't know sweetie.

        (As Desera lies on her back.)

                    DESERA
I notice that all the tress have a glow that
catches all our eyes.

        (Traci and Ebony burst out in laughter.)

                    DESERA
I am completely taken away by the trees because
they all possess strength and perseverance.

(Desera daydreams about how her mom, Traci,
Ebony, and she have come a long way. She
looks over at her sisters and kisses their
foreheads.)

                    DESERA
Hey Traci and Ebony, what do ya'll like about
the trees?

        (Traci rolls over and hugs Desera.)

                    TRACI
I like the colors and the smell. The trees
remind me of Grandma's pancakes with warm
maple syrup.

                    EBONY
They remind me of Grandma Jada's Blackberry
ice tea.

                    DESERA
Well, these trees remind me of Grandma's sweet
Blackberry pie and her warm Maple biscuits.

                    TRACI
Yeah, I miss her smile.

                    EBONY
I really miss her laughter and her jokes.

                DESERA
I think that Grandma Jada is looking down on
us from heaven and smiling.

                TRACI
I think grandma is watching over us and will
always be with us.

ACT ONE SCENE TWO A living room

> (Janelle and her family are sitting on a three piece teal sectional, with a large black rectangular ottoman. There are high white voltage ceilings with a black and silver glassed fireplace.)

(Janelle reaches for her cup of Hazel Nut coffee and takes a sip. She sits her cup of coffee down on the dark oat coffee table. Then she glances at Desera.)

> JANELLE

Hey Desera, what are you thinking about so hard? Would you like a cup of Hazel Nut coffee?

(Desera shrugs her shoulders, and sways her multi-colored notebook from left to right and sighs.)

> DESERA

I am just thinking about my life and my future.

(Desera plops herself next to Janelle and leans her head on Janelle's right shoulder.)

> DESERA

Mom, I just feel like I'm coming to a crossroad in my life. (She sighs.)

                    DESERA

I mean, I'm twenty-seven years old and I have
no clue as to what I want to do with my life.
It's like I have so many things that I want to
accomplish, but deep inside I feel empty. I'm
missing something in my life.

          (She glances up at Janelle and smiles.)

                    DESERA

I have so many things that are bottled up
inside. My mind is constantly racing and all I
can do is pick up my pen and write.

          (Janelle kisses Desera's forehead.)

                    JANELLE

Well, sweetie, you're a young beautiful and
intelligent woman. You can do anything that
you put your mind to.

(Janelle squeezes Desera. Then she glances
over at Ebony.)

                    JANELLE

Hey Ebony, is everything ok? You're too quiet
and you're not joking around like you usually
do. It's not like you not to talk.

(Ebony is in an Indian style position holding
a white and pink composition book. As she
glances out the large oval window, she writes
about the beautiful scenery in the backyard.)

EBONY

I was just wondering if through my hazel eyes I can see things in different colors. I decided to write about the beautiful scenery in the backyard as I see it.

(Ebony smiles. Her eyes make contact with Janelle. She sighs.)

EBONY

I'm good, I'm just thinking about what I want to say. Suddenly I feel the words flowing like rain.

(As she presses her yellow and black happy face pen onto the white page, the words begin to flow out like rain.)

(Janelle comes over and sits next to Traci.)

JANELLE

Hey sweetie, how are you doing? What are you painting?

(Traci glances up at Janelle and smiles.)

TRACI

I'm fine. I'm just painting trees and the lake in the backyard. Mom do you think that someday I'll be a great artist?

JANELLE

Of course, you'll be an excellent artist. You should follow your heart and pursue your dreams.

(Traci hugs Janelle. Then Desera and Ebony shuffles over to the couch and puts her arms around the both of them.)

ACT ONE SCENE THREE Desera's Bedroom.

> (The room is large with pink walls. Desera's large light oak queen canopy bed is decorated with a pink and black striped comforter. There are two large white trimmed rectangular windows.)

(As Desera lies on her back on her soft bed, the sun peaks through the white trimmed rectangular window onto Desera's cinnamon brown face. Her reflection in the window reveals her beauty. Desera turns over onto her right side and turns her silver and black radio on. She rolls onto her back, grabs her pink ball point pen, and begins writing.)

(The DJ Styles speaks in a low brass tone.)

DJ STYLES
Hey ATL this is DJ Styles, ATL finest, and you're listening to Flavor 450, the station that always play all of your favorite Hip-Hop and R&B songs every day.

DJ STYLES
Okay, the first caller is on the line. DJ Styles pauses, and then proceeds. Okay caller number one, you're on the air.

CALLER #1
Yes, my name is Tameka and I would like for you to play *"Blackberry Molasses"* by *Mista*.

                    DJ STYLES
Alright Tameka, I'll get your request in. Now
tell the people of Atlanta, what your favorite
station is.

                    CALLER #1
Flavor 450.

The song begins.

                    DESERA
As I begin to write, my thoughts begin pouring
out like rain showers. The words on the paper
illustrate my deep passion for my gift of
writing. My racing thoughts make the pink pen
sound as if a violinist is performing at the
Julliard School of Arts.

The song continues.

                    DESERA
I begin pouring out my feelings onto the white
page as though I'm painting a picture of a
violent storm that rushes through a valley
filled with various sunflowers.

                    DESERA
I am painting a visual picture of a woman that
has kept her true feelings bottled up. This
strong woman is finally free to pour out her
feelings that have been lying dormant inside
of her heart.

The song ends.

DESERA

How I know, you may wonder. I know because I am that woman. My pain within my broken soul is deep like a bloody gnash that a little child receives after falling off of his or her bike.

(Desera sighs and continues.)

DESERA

You see my friends; I mourn as a way of coping with situations that I have had to endure in the past. Unforgettable situations in my life have left me, feeling lonely, afraid, confused, and angry. My tears of sorrow are only for a season. I know that someday I will laugh again and change people's lives.

ACT ONE SCENE FOUR Julie's front patio.

>(There are Blackberry trees surrounding
>her light sandy brown square stone patio.
>Following a yellow and a blue patio set.
>The grass is emerald green and filled
>with sunflowers.)

(Julie and Desera are sitting on two yellow
and blue lounge chairs that are faced across
from each other, sipping on sweet lemonade.)

                DESERA
The swift wind causes the various Japanese
maple trees such as Butterfly, Crimson Queen,
and Sherwood Flame leaves to fall *like light
rain showers* on a sunny day.

(Desera reaches over onto her right side and
grabs her notebook, she discovers Maple leaves
in the center of it.)

(Julie lies on her yellow and blue lounge chair.
As she sips on her freshly squeezed lemonade,
she glances over at Desera and smiles.)

                JULIE
So girl, how have you been?

(Desera glances up at Julie and smiles.)

                DESERA

I'm good. I've been writing a lot. Trying to figure out what I want to do as far as having a job, my own place, and etc.

                    JULIE
Wow, that's awesome.

                    DESERA
Yeah, it is.

                    JULIE
You should send your story to "*The New York Star.*"

(Julie shuffles into the house, grabs her lap top and glides back to her lounge chair. As she sits in an Indian style position, Desera grabs her notebook and sits by Julie.)

(Desera verbally tells Julie her story. As Julie and Desera finishes up, Desera hugs her.)

                    DESERA
Well, enough about me. How are things going with you?

                    JULIE
Things are good. I've been working at the "*Epiphany Café.*"

                    DESERA

Sweet! Do you like working at *"Epiphany's."*

                    JULIE
Yes. It has a nice atmosphere to it.

                    DESERA
Congratulations girl! It appears that you're
doing well for yourself.

                    JULIE
Thanks girl! You should come by. We can eat
and chat.

                    DESERA
Okay, I will. I better get going and see if my
mom needs anything before I head home. Thanks
for everything.

(Desera hugs Julie and her phones rings.
Desera glances at her phone and sees that it's
Janelle.)

                    DESERA
Oh . . . its my mom, Janelle calling.

ACT ONE SCENE FIVE Melanie's office.

> (The large rectangular office with high windows captures the beautiful city of New York. The navy blue and white stripped wall brings color and liveliness to the room. Followed by a dark brown three-piece office set that is covered with large stacks of papers.)

(Melanie is sitting at her large rectangular desk sipping on her Hazel Nut coffee. As she glances down, she notices a message on her laptop. Melanie opens her e-mail and begins reading.)

MELANIE
To Whom It May Concern: Life is a choice and a privilege that we as individuals have.

(As Melanie ponders on the first sentence. She raises her left eyebrow and continues reading.)

MELANIE
It is something that we must not take for granted. My words on the page are beginning to flow like a water fall . . . they are coming so fast almost like title waves in an ocean.

MELANIE
It's a special gift that God has granted us and we should make the most of it while we're on this earth.

(Melanie's eyes are captured by the words on the screen, and she can hear Desera's voice.)

       MELANIE

Life is a journey in which we find ourselves on various emotional roller-coasters.

(Melanie sips her Hazel Nut coffee, then continues reading.)

       MELANIE

Soul searching and growing pains are just a taste of the many trails and tests that we endure as human beings.

(Melanie ponders and then continues.)

       MELANIE

No matter what challenges that we may face throughout our lives, we can make it through.

      (Melanie sips her Hazel Nut coffee.)

       MELANIE

Take my life as example; I'm a 27 year old African American woman who has endured the sharp pains of physical abuse.

      (Melanie twirls her pen.)

MELANIE

Shedding many tears of sorrow and pain from my
father's large cinnamon brown rough hands that
has left my left eye black and blue.

(Melanie scrolls down and continues reading.)

MELANIE

I can remember as a little girl comforting my
younger twin sisters Ebony and Traci as we
watched our parents fight like Ike and Tina
Turner.

(Melanie nods her head.)

MELANIE

You see, I wrote this letter not because I'm
looking for sympathy, but to encourage people
in similar situations that, there's always
hope. As long as there is breath in their
body, he or she will have many opportunities
for situations in their life to change.

ACT ONE SCENE SIX Brandon's restaurant "Eddie Lee's Soul food."

(It's somewhere in downtown Atlanta Georgia. There's a large cursive red sign that says, *"Welcome to Eddie Lee's Soul food."* Inside the red champagne café' *there are round glass tables.*)

(As Desera waits to be seated, she notices . . .)

> DESERA
>
> *Oh, what a wonderful tribute to all of the famous Jazz musicians Miles Davis, Billie Holiday, Louis Armstrong, Earl Hines, Duke Ellington, Sidney Bechet, Sarah Vaughan,* and Nat King Cole. I do believe you have on display more than 100 pictures Jazz artist!!!

(The host takes Desera to her table.)

(Desera glances around the restaurant and is fascinated with the pictures of various Jazz Musicians.)

(As Desera admires the famous artists, Brandon slowly comes up to the table.)

> BRANDON
>
> Hello, can I start you out with an appetizer, Ma'am?

(Desera sighs.)

                    DESERA
What do you recommend?

          (Desera glances up and smiles.)

                    DESERA
Hey Brandon, how are you? I really like your
Uncle Eddie's restaurant.

                    BRANDON
I'm good. My Uncle Eddie and I have been
doing well. We have been bringing in a lot
of business since we started serving homemade
Blackberry pie and our special breakfast
"Chicken and Waffles" which are served with
sweet Molasses.

                    DESERA
Well, I think I'll have the "Chicken and
Waffles" special please.

                    BRANDON
Aright. So how have you been?

                    DESERA
I've been good. I have been writing a lot
about myself. I'm trying to figure out my life
as far as career wise and etc. I sent an email
to the Editor of *The New York Star*" inquiring
about being a Journal Analyst.

                    BRANDON
That's wonderful Desera. When do you think
you'll hear back from the Editor?

                    DESERA
Hopefully soon.

        (Brandon smiles at Desera.)

(Desera take a sip of her sweet tea, while
Brandon gets her food.)

        (Brandon returns with Desera's order.)

                    BRANDON
I'm sure you'll get the Journal Analyst job.

                    DESERA
Thanks, I'm sure you and your Uncle Eddie will
continue to have a successful business at this
fine restaurant.

                    BRANDON
Thanks.

(Brandon hugs Desera. Then Desera's phone
rings.)

ACT ONE SCENE SEVEN Stefanie's Apartment.

(Stefanie and Desera are sitting on Stefanie's leopard couch. Desera glances up at her laptop and notices an email message from the CEO of *The New York Star.*)

DESERA

Oh . . . I have an email from Melanie Williams the CEO of *The New York Star.*

(Before Desera attempts to open the e-mail, she pauses and smiles at Stefanie.)

(Stefanie sighs.)

STEFANIE

What?

DESERA

Well, I wrote to an anonymous person at *The New York Star.*

STEFANIE

Wow! Really? What position did you ask for?

DESERA

Journal Analyst.

STEFANIE

Well, maybe you should check your e-mail.

(Desera's bites her bottom lip.)

(Then she pauses for a moment as if she's in deep thought.)

> (Stefanie reaches across Desera and clicks on the e-mail that reads Melanie Williams.)

> (Desera's palms are sweaty. She glances at Stefanie and smiles. Then Desera become excited and begins reading.)

Desera

Its an email from Melanie Williams!!!

Desera (read out loud)

Dear Desera Harrison,
Hello, my name is Melanie Williams and I'm a representative/ CEO of "The New York Star." I was really moved by your letter because I could hear the pain and passion in your voice. Reading your story has really opened my eyes to life and the struggles which people endure in their lives. The story is not only about you, it's about many women like yourself. The strong voice in your letter represents many women who have experienced or are currently in abusive situations. Your passion in your writing reveals your strengths, weaknesses, storms, and victories, in which at one point or another everyone has gone through. Your voice is strong. You paint pictures of your

storming past. You uplift and encourage us with your defining moment, where you decide to keep pursuing your dreams, despite your past which has made you stronger. Your voice represents women who are victims of domestic violence. Your positive outlook on life reveals your confidence and determination to make it despite life's adversities. This mention of you being abuse is lively and will touch the hearts of women. You being a strong woman that protects your love ones from harm really captured my attention because it shows your strength, perseverance, and ability to lead. Ms. Desera Harrison your letter has not only touched my heart, but has proven that you have what it takes to become a full-time Journal Analyst. Sincerely, Melanie Williams.

(Desera and Stefanie scream, and jump up and down.)

                    DESERA
Yeah, I'm going to call my mom.

ACT ONE SCENE EIGHT Ebony and Traci's Bedroom.

>(Their large rectangular room is painted half pink and lavender. Ebony's side has a pink rug, lamp, desk, and chair. Ebony has her writings that she composes in a large pink notebook on her desk. She also has a light pink canopy bed. On Traci side of the room she has lavender bedding, rug, desk, lamp, and a chair.)

(Ebony's sitting at her desk with her pink flowery pen writing away.)

>(She glances over at Traci.)

(Traci's standing graciously by her diamond shaped window, painting on her white canvas. She paints a Blackberry and a Maple tree.)

>(Ebony smiles.)

>EBONY

Hey I love your painting.

>TRACI

Thanks. It's a Blackberry and a Maple tree.

>EBONY

Nice.

(Ebony pauses, sighs, and continues writing.)

31

                TRACI
So Ebony, what are you writing about?

        (Ebony raises her right eyebrow.)

                EBONY
Our family.

        (Traci smiles.)

                TRACI
Cool.

(Traci walks over to Ebony and sits on her
pink bed.)

                EBONY
Hey Traci, do you ever think about Daddy?

        (Traci frowns.)

                TRACI
Sometimes, I guess. I try not to think about
him a lot.

(Ebony walks over to Traci and hugs her.)

                EBONY
Why not?

                TRACI
I just don't understand why he hurt Mom and
Desera.

EBONY
Me either, but Daddy's gone.

(Ebony lowers her eyes.)

(Traci lifts Ebony's head up and hugs her.)

TRACI
I know he is. Now it's just you, Desera, Mom, and I.

ACT TWO SCENE ONE Desera's office July 2008-Summer.

(Located at "*The New York Star*" Headquarters.)

        DESERA
I find that despite the usual daily chaotic work atmosphere, I am able to work with little or no distractions.

(Desera has large rectangular blue and white walls. She has a red oak desk with a dark brown leather chair.)

(As Desera is typing away on her computer, she notices an image on her computer.)

        (She turns around.)

(A Journal Analyst stands outside the door.)

        (Desera waves.)

        DESERA
You can come in.

        (Desera smiles, stands, and introduces herself.)

        DESERA
Hello, I'm Desera, it's nice to meet you.

        (Staci shakes her hands and smiles.)

                    STACI

Hi, I'm Staci. I'm one of the Journal Analyst
here. If you have any questions or concerns
don't hesitate to ask. I'm right next door.

(Desera takes a sip of her Hazel Nut coffee,
types a couple of sentences, and glances up.)

                    DESERA

Well, thanks for making me feel welcome. This
is my first day and I'm from Atlanta Georgia.
My mom, Janelle, and my twin sisters, Ebony
and Traci moved up here with me. My mom and my
sisters live six doors down from me.

                    STACI

Glad to have you here. We should go out for
coffee and Blackberry pie sometimes.

                    DESERA

Alright, that sounds good.

(Desera rises from her desk and shakes Staci's
hand. Staci walks towards the door and pauses.
She faces Desera.)

                    STACI

Hey Desera, do you want to go out for coffee
Thursday at "*The Olympia Café*" at around six?

                    DESERA

Yeah sure.

                STACI
See you there.

(Staci exits Desera's office.)

(Desera notices a tall handsome man as she quietly shuts her door and smiles to herself.)

ACT TWO SCENE TWO Janelle's beauty shop "New Beginnings."

(This salon is located in New York City. This salon is large and has high recess lights that transforms the room into a spa.)

(Janelle is running back and forth from the shampoo bowl to the front desk taking walk-in appointments.)

(As Janelle is escorting clients to her station, Desera rushes in.)

(Janelle has her hands tied.)

(Desera pauses. She sighs.)

(Desera softly pats Janelle on the shoulder.)

DESERA
Hey Mom, can I help you with anything?

JANELLE
Thanks sweetie. Yes, you can help me shampoo my clients.

DESERA
Alright, no problem.

(Desera escorts one of the clients back to the shampoo bowl.)

(As one of the hairstylists walks in, Janelle sighs.)

> JANELLE
Thanks Erika. Finally, I can relax.

> (Janelle glides back to her station and slumps down into the chair. She untwists the cap off of her Pepsi and takes a sip.)

> (Desera has finished her first client and summons for another to come back to shampoo bowl.)

(Janelle makes her way over to the shampoo bowl next to Desera.)

> (Janelle smiles at Desera and hugs her.)

> JANELLE
Thanks Desera for helping me out with my clients.

> DESERA
No problem. Hey Mom, you won't believe what just happened to me today.

> JANELLE
What sweetie?

DESERA

Okay, today I saw this incredible man who works at *"The New York Star."* I don't know his name and I haven't met him yet, but I would like too.

(Janelle smiles and chuckles.)

JANELLE

Well, by the way your face lights up, I can tell that you like this mystery man.

DESERA (Desera smiles.)

Maybe a little.

ACT TWO SCENE THREE "The Olympia Café.

> (In downtown New York there's an oval lifted cursive red sign which reads *"The Olympia Cafe." Inside the café, there are blue and red booths* with round black and silver tables.)

(Its ten minutes to six and Desera rushes in the door drenched with rain.)

(While Desera attempts to shut her green and blue umbrella, Stacie summons her over to her table.)

            STACI
Hey, I'm glad you made it.

            DESERA
Yeah, me too.

            STACI
Well Desera, what are you in the mood for?

            (The waiter scrolls up to their table.)

            KEVIN
Hello ladies, my name is Kevin and I'll be your waiter for tonight. May I start you off with something to drink?

            DESERA
Sure, I would like a Strawberry daiquiri.

                    KEVIN
And for you Ms.?

                    STACI
I will have a Cosmo.

(Kevin hands Desera and Staci their menus. They
seemed a little undecided.)

                    KEVIN
Okay ladies, I'll give you two a couple of
minutes to decide what you want.

                    DESERA
Thanks.

        (Staci takes a sip of her Cosmo.)

                    STACI
So Desera, what do you want to eat?

                    DESERA
I don't know. What do you recommend?

                    STACI
Well, their burgers are excellent.

                    DESERA
Okay, I'll try the bacon cheddar burger.

                    STACI
Good choice. Me too.

KEVIN (Kevin returns.)
You ladies ready to order?

        DESERA
We both want the bacon cheddar burger.

        STACI
So how do you like working for "*The New York Star?*"

        DESERA
Well, this is my first week, but so far I like it.

        STACI
Great.

    (Kevin returns with the food.)

(Desera raises her glass and makes a toast.)

        DESERA
Here's to my new job, success, and happiness.

ACT TWO SCENE FOUR Janelle's Apartment.

(As Janelle and her twin daughters Ebony and Traci unpack and get settled in, Janelle notices a tall brown skinned man walking past her front door wearing a white dress shirt with light denim-jeans and white Jordan's.)

(Janelle smiles to herself and then calls Ebony and Traci.)

                    JANELLE
Ebony and Traci, can you come help me unpack some of these boxes?

        (Ebony and Traci zoom to the kitchen.)

                    EBONY
Yes Mom.

(Traci grabs Janelle waist and squeezes her tightly.)

                    TRACI
Hey Mom, I love my room!

        (Ebony kisses Janelle on her left check.)

                    EBONY
I love my room too Mommy!

(Janelle kisses each of them on the forehead.)

JANELLE

I'm glad. Can you two start unpacking these boxes, while I run out to the car to get something?

EBONY

Okay.

        (Traci smiles.)

TRACI

Sure.

(As Janelle makes her way to her car, she comes across the same man who she saw walking past her front door.)

(The man walks over to Janelle, introduces himself, and smiles.)

KEVIN

Hello, my name is Kevin. I live two floors down from you.

        (Janelle pauses and smiles.)

JANELLE

Hello, I'm Janelle.

KEVIN

Nice to meet you. When did you move here?

JANELLE

Oh about two weeks ago. My three daughters and I are from Atlanta Georgia. My oldest daughter Desera was offered a job at "*The New York Star*" as a Journal Analyst. I have opened my own beauty shop called "*New Beginnings.*"

KEVIN

Well, I'm a waiter at "The Olympia Café.'"

JANELLE

Alright, maybe my daughters and I will dine there sometimes.

KEVIN

Can I have your number?

JANELLE

Sure, its . . .

(She mouths the number and Kevin hugs Janelle.)

KEVIN

Well, I hate to cut this conversation short but I have to get ready for work.

(Janelle smiles.)

JANELLE

Okay, talk to you later. Ebony and Traci, I'm coming, I haven't forgotten about you all.

ACT TWO SCENE FIVE Desera's apartment.

(Desera is sitting on her red and white couch sipping sweet ice tea. She's relaxing and watching a movie called "*My Sister's Keeper*" with Ebony and Traci.)

(As Ebony and Traci are lying next to Desera, her cell phone rings.)

DESERA

Hey Mom!

JANELLE

Hey, how are ya'll doing?

(Ebony and Traci yell.)

EBONY AND TRACI

Hey Mom!

(Desera and Janelle laughs.)

(Desera glances up at Ebony and places her pointer finger to her mouth.)

DESERA

Hey shh . . . Mommy and I are trying to talk.

JANELLE

Well yesterday, I met a nice man named Kevin. He works at "*The Olympia Café'*."

DESERA

Oh yes, Kevin, he was me and my co-worker Staci's waiter.

(JANELLE smiles.)

JANELLE

Really! What's your opinion of him?

DESERA

He seems nice. So how do you feel about him?

JANELLE

He's nice. Well, I saw Kevin passing by my front door but I met Kevin outside of our apartment complex.

(Desera smiles.)

DESERA

So did you give Kevin your number?

JANELLE

Yes, I did, and girl he called me that same night. We talked on the phone for about five hours.

DESERA

Oh my God Mom, that's great! So when are you all going out? I assume you two are going to go out right. Kevin seems like a nice stable mature man. He's employed which is a major plus and he's very attractive for an older man.

(Janelle smiles and chuckles.)

JANELLE

Oh, ok, um . . . an older man, now I'm old. No honey, I'm grown and sexy. Tonight we're going out to *"The Olympia Café.'"*

(Ebony grabs the phone.)

EBONY

Hey Mommy!

(Traci picks up the other phone.)

TRACI

Hey Mommy! Are you coming to pick us up?

JANELLE

Well babies, I'm going on a date with a nice man named Kevin and I am bringing him by around six so you both can meet him.

EBONY AND TRACI

Okay Mommy. Love you!

ACT TWO SCENE SIX: Desera's apartment. "The Olympia Café'."

(Janelle and Kevin are at Desera's apartment. Ebony and Traci begin warming up to him after they asked him various questions. Then Kevin and Janelle dine in at *The Olympia Café'.*)

(Desera hugs Kevin.)

DESERA
Hey Kevin, nice to see you again.

(Janelle introduces Kevin to Ebony and Traci.)

JANELLE
Girls, this is my friend Kevin.

EBONY
Hi, I'm Ebony. Where are you taking my mom out to? Do you like my mom?

KEVIN (Smiles)
It is nice to meet you. To answer your question yes, I do like your mom, and we're going to *"The Olympia Café'."*

TRACI
Hi, I'm Traci, where do you work? How did you two meet? Are you married?

                JANELLE (Blushes)
Traci and Ebony get over here and sit down.

                KEVIN
It's all right Janelle; I do like you.

JANELLE (smiles)
Well, we are getting ready to go.

                DESERA EBONY TRACI
Bye Mom!

                JANELLE
Bye girls. Be good for Desera.

(Janelle and Kevin are at *"The Olympia Café'"*
sipping white wine and laughing. As they're
eating their food, jazz music sets the mood in
the place.)

                JANELLE
Kevin, I love this restaurant. It is very
classy and romantic. It looks very expensive.
You don't have to pay if you don't want to.

                KEVIN
I got the bill.

                JANELLE
You sure.

                    KEVIN
I'm positive. Don't worry, I'm good for it.
Remember I work here.

                    JANELLE
Alright, thanks.

                    KEVIN
So what's a beautiful woman like yourself doing
single?

          (Janelle sighs.)

                    JANELLE
Well five years ago, my ex-husband Anthony
left me and the children. He was physically
abusive to Desera and me but he never put his
hands on Ebony and Traci. Well enough about
me. What about you?

          (Kevin reaches for Janelle's right hand.)

                    KEVIN
Hey, I think you're a strong woman who deserves
to be treated like a queen. Well, I'm single and
I don't have any kids, but I love children.

                    JANELLE
Alright, that's good to know.

                    KEVIN
I know that we just met but I would like to
see you again sometimes.

                    JANELLE
Yeah sure.

                    KEVIN
Is next Saturday night okay?

                    JANELLE
Sure.

        (After dinner, Kevin takes Janelle to
        her apartment. As Janelle reaches in her
        black and gray Coach bag for her keys,
        Kevin smiles.)

                    KEVIN
Well Janelle, I really had a great time.

                    JANELLE
Me too.

        (Janelle sighs.)

                    JANELLE
Kevin, would you like to go to Traci's art show
at her Professional Performing Arts School in
New York, New York.

                    KEVIN
Sure. When is it?

                    JANELLE
It's next Wednesday night at seven.

                KEVIN
Great.

        (Kevin hugs Janelle.)

        (Janelle smiles.)

                JANELLE
Well, I guess I'll see you Wednesday.

(As Janelle turns the door knob, Ebony and
Traci rushes to the door.)

        (They both hug her.)

ACT TWO SCENE SEVEN (Professional Performing Arts School)

(There's a large sky blue art studio which displays all the students artwork. Janelle and Kevin are enjoying one another's company as they are strolling around the studio, admiring all the artwork.)

JANELLE

I want to thank you for coming with me and the girls to Traci's art show. It means a lot to me.

KEVIN

You're welcome. I really enjoy being around you.

JANELLE

Really? Why?

KEVIN

Well, for one you're a family person, you love your children unconditionally, and you're humble. It's hard to find these qualities in a woman.

JANELLE

Thanks for the compliment. I want to know more about you.

                    KEVIN

Well, I'm a simple person. It doesn't take a
lot for me to be happy. I'm very protective
and loving.

                    JANELLE

Me too.

                    KEVIN

I'm a good listener and an excellent cook. I
would like to cook for you and your girls one
day.

                    JANELLE

Alright.

(The Art judges have finished making their rounds
around the studio and have come to a decision.)

        (Ms. Freeman clears her throat and speaks
        into the microphone.)

                    MS. FREEMAN

Good evening everyone. I would like to thank
each and every one of you for coming out
tonight. Well, let's get the show started. This
is the Professional Performing Arts School"
Annual Art Show's 52nd anniversary. Each year
we encourage our students to illustrate their
art ability. First of all, I think we all
should give all of the contestants a round of
applause.

(The audience arise and applauses the students.)

(Mrs. Freeman summons the audiences to take their seats and continues.)

MS. FREEMAN

Well the judges have carefully observed all of the amazing artwork and have made a group decision.

(As Ms. Freeman slowly opens the white envelop, Janelle clenches Kevin's hand tightly.)

JANELLE

I feel my heart's racing. Oh . . . Kevin I am sorry. Was I squeezing your hand?

(Janelle becomes excited as she hears . . .)

MS. FREEMAN

And the winner of the 52nd Annual Art show for the fall 2008 school year is Traci Harrison.

(Janelle and Kevin leap for joy.) (Desera and Ebony scream.)

DESERA

Go Traci!

EBONY

Yeah Traci!

(Janelle, Desera, and Ebony make their way to Traci to hug her.)

                    KEVIN
Congratulations Traci. I would like to take you all out to Baskin Robins if it's alright with your Mom.

                    JANELLE
Sure.

ACT THREE SCENE ONE (Annual Christmas Party. December 2008)

> (Everyone is dressed in black and white attire. The holiday spirit is defiantly in the atmosphere. *"The New York Star"* Headquarters looks like a Winter Wonderland with all the white confetti, the large white snowflakes, multi-colored Christmas lights, and various gourmet foods.)

(Desera is wearing a black tube top dress and three inch heel shoes.)

(As Desera mingles with some of her co-workers, Staci and Derek make their way over to her.)

(Staci's wearing a short black cocktail feather dress with four inch heels. Staci and her good friend Derek walks up to Desera. Staci hugs Desera.)

> STACI
> Hey Desera, you look nice.

> DESERA
> Thanks Staci. So do you.

> STACI
> Desera, I want you to meet my good friend Derek.

(Desera and Derek shake hands.)

                    DESERA
Hi, nice to meet you.

          (Staci nudges Desera.)

                    STACI
Well, I'll leave you two alone.

                    DEREK
You too. How do you like working here so far?

                    DESERA
I like it a lot. Working here is exciting and
it's something that I always wanted to do. How
long have you been working here?

                    DEREK
Oh about two years. I have been living here
practically all of my life.

                    DESERA
Oh, ok, I'm from Atlanta Georgia and I wrote
Melanie Williams a letter about getting a job
position here.

                    DEREK
Alright, you're beautiful.

          (Desera smiles and blushes.)

                    DESERA
Thanks. You're good looking yourself.

                    DEREK
Are you single?

                    DESERA
Yes I am. How about you?

                    DEREK
Yes, I am.

          (Desera smiles.)

                    DESERA
Alright.

                    DEREK
Maybe we can go out sometimes.

                    DESERA
Alright.

                    DEREK
How about next Friday night?

                    DESERA
Friday sounds good.

          (Then Desera and Derek exchange numbers.)

ACT TRREE SCENE TWO "The New York Star" Headquarters January 2009.

> (Desera is sitting at her desk and the only sound that is present is her fingers tapping on the keyboard. She's working on her story entitled "*Blackberry Molasses,*" *an* inspiring story about women who have endured physical abuse such as herself.)

(While Desera finishes up her two sentences, Derek knocks on her door.)

(Desera glances up.)

DESERA
Hey, how are you doing?

DEREK(Derek walks in.)
Fine. It was nice seeing you last week.

DESERA
You too.

DEREK
What are you working on?

DESERA
A story called "*Blackberry Molasses*" which tells a story about women who have endured physical abuse such as myself.

                    DEREK
Well, I believe your story will inspire women
and give them strength to leave from a bad
environment and move on.

                    DESERA
Yeah, I think so. I mean, I just want women
in abusive situations to know that they have
a voice that needs to be heard, and I want to
encourage them to leave.

                    DEREK
Cool. Well, I have to get back to work. Are we
still on for Friday?

                    DESERA
Yes.

ACT THREE SCENE THREE "The restaurant "Epiphany's."

(Desera and Derek are enjoying dinner and laughing. The lights are dim and there's Contemporary Jazz playing in the background.)

(While Desera and Derek are eating, Julie comes over.)

(Desera and Derek laugh.)

(Then Desera glances up and notices Julie.)

(Desera stands and hugs Julie.)

                    DESERA
Hey Julie, this is Derek.

                    JULIE
Nice to meet you.

                    DEREK
Same here.

                    DESERA
I didn't know that you moved to New York. When did you move out here?

                    JULIE
Oh, about three months ago.

                    DESERA
Well, I'm happy you're here.

        (Julie hugs Desera.)

                    JULIE
I better get back to work. Bye girl and it
was nice meeting you Derek. I'm sure I'll be
seeing more of you. (Julie leaves.)

                    DEREK
Your friend's nice.

                    DESERA
Yes she is. Well, I almost forgot to thank you
for dinner.

        (Derek gently grabs her left hand.)

                    DEREK
You're welcome.

                    DESERA
So what do you like to do for fun?

                    DEREK
I like pretty much anything. Going to the
movies, going bowling, writing poetry, playing
basketball, playing the piano and saxophone,
and chilling with friends. I love spending time
with my mom and my younger sister Destiny.

                    DESERA
Well, I think that's wonderful Derek.

                    DEREK
What do you enjoy doing?

                    DESERA
I enjoy going to the beach, spending time with
my family, writing, watching movies, and etc.
I'm very optimistic and laidback. Sometimes
I'm shy and sensitive but I'm also outgoing.

                    DEREK
You have wonderful qualities Desera. We should
do this again. I really like you and I enjoy
your company.

                    DESERA
Thanks. I like your company as well. You're
easy to talk to.

(The waiter comes back with Derek's credit
card.)

                    DEREK
Well, are you ready to go?

                    DESERA
Yes.

         (Then Desera and Derek leave.)

ACT THREE SCENE FOUR Janelle's apartment Mid January 2009.

> (Janelle, Ebony, Traci, and Kevin are in the red and white kitchen making lasagna from scratch and baking chocolate chip cookies. The door bell rings. Traci runs to the door smiling. When Traci opens the door, Desera and Derek hug her.)

(Janelle shuffles over to Desera and Derek.)

(Desera introduces Derek.)

DESERA
Derek this is mom Janelle.

DEREK (hugs Janelle.)
Nice to meet you.

JANELLE
Same here. Desera, he's good looking.

DESERA (Blushes.)
This is my mom's friend Kevin.

KEVIN
Nice to meet you.

DEREK
Hey, I've seen you at "*The Olympia Café'*" couples of times.

                    KEVIN
Well, actually I'm a waiter at *"The Olympia
Café'."* I've been working there for three
years.

                    DEREK
Good. Well, I work at *"The New York Star"* as a
Journal Analyst along with Desera.

DESERA (Smiles.)
Derek, these are my twin sisters, Ebony and
Traci.

                    EBONY
Hey.

                    TRACI
Hi.

                    DEREK
Nice to meet you both.

                    DESERA
And last but not least my Grandparents Roger
and Evette.

          (Derek shakes their hands.)

                    DEREK
Hello, how are you?

GRANDMA EVETTE

I'm doing well. My husband Roger and I are from Atlanta Georgia. We're thinking about staying in New York so we can be closer to our daughter Janelle and our grandchildren.

GRANDPA ROGER

This is my third time being in New York City. When I was young, I went to Harlem New York with my father once a month. I remember having to help my dad clean *"The Apollo Theater." We* always watched the comedy acts and sometimes we would meet some of the comedians.

DEREK

Well, that's seems exciting. I can't even imagine what it must have felt like to witness black talent.

(Desera shuffles over to Grandpa Roger and hugs him.)

(Janelle heads toward the stove to take the large pan of lasagna out and places it on the kitchen table.)

(Everyone's gathered around the large glass table.)

ACT THREE SCENE FIVE The "New York Star".

>   (Derek brings his mother Cassie to work
>   to met Desera. Desera's computer keys
>   sounded as if, a rain shower was pouring
>   down into an endless pit.)

(As Desera continues typing, she hears a knock
at her door.)

>   (Desera raises her head.)

(Then Desera summons Derek and Cassie to come
in.)

>   (Derek and his mother stroll over to
>   Desera's desk and introduce Cassie.)

(Desera slowly rises and kisses Derek.)

>   DEREK
Hey babe, this is my mother Cassie.

>   (Desera rises and shakes Cassie left hand.)

>   DESERA
It's nice to meet you. I see where Derek gets
his good looks from.

CASSIE (Cassie smiles.)
Thanks. Derek tells me you're an extraordinary
writer.

DESERA

Thanks. I try to express myself in a way where everyone can relate to what I'm writing about at that particular time.

CASSIE

Amazing. I wish I had the gift of writing. I know from reading Derek's articles in the paper that you defiantly have to love what you do.

DESERA

I agree.

DEREK

Well Desera, would you like to go to lunch with my Mom and I?

DESERA

Sure! Let me run my report to Melanie first.

(Desera knocks on the door.)

(Melanie summons her in.)

(Desera hands Melanie her story called *"Freeing The Inner Self."*)

MELANIE

Thanks Desera.

DESERA

No problem.

                    MELANIE
By the way, good job Desera.

                    DESERA
Thanks.

        (Desera shuffles back to her office.)

        (Her phone rings.)

                    DESERA
Hello, oh hi Mom. Hey I'm about to go lunch
with Derek and his mom Cassie. I'll call you
back later. Love you, bye.

        (Desera hangs up the phone.)

ACT THREE SCENE SIX Central Park April 2009.

(It's a sunny day in New York City. Janelle and Kevin are taking a scroll in the park. As Janelle and Kevin are enjoying each other's company, Kevin gets down on one knee and proposes to Janelle.)

DESERA

It's mid April, Janelle and Kevin have been together for eight months. During this time period Janelle and Kevin have become really close. We really enjoy Kevin's company. We all like the way he treats Janelle. I am so happy for Janelle and Kevin.

(As Kevin and Janelle are enjoying the view of the lake and it's fresh misty water fountain, Kevin gazes into Janelle eyes and holds her right hand.)

KEVIN

Janelle, do you love me?

JANELLE

Yes.

(Kevin gets on one knee.)

KEVIN

Then will you marry me?

                    JANELLE (Sighs and smiles.)
Yes!

                    KEVIN (Hugs and kisses Janelle.)

                    KEVIN
Yes!

                    JANELLE
I have to call Desera.

                    KEVIN
Okay.

        (Janelle hugs Kevin.)

                    JANELLE
I'm so happy baby. Oh my God, let me call
Desera.

                    KEVIN
Alright, I think I'll call my mom.

        (Janelle phone rings.)

                    JANELLE
Yeah Desera, guess what, Kevin and I are
engaged.

        (Desera screams.)

        (Kevin calls his mom.)

            KEVIN
Hello mom, Janelle said yes to my proposal.

    (Kevin's mom, screams.)

            JANELLE
Well Desera, I'll talk to you later. I love
you.

            KEVIN
Love you mom. I'll talk to you later. Bye.

        Kevin (He hangs up.)
My mom's excited. She was screaming in my ear.

            JANELLE
Desera was the same way.

            KEVIN
I love you.

            JANELLE
Baby, I love you too.

            KEVIN
Well, can we walk over onto the grass? There
I have set up a picnic table.

(Kevin and Janelle sit down on the red and white
picnic table with a basket filled with various
fruits and a bottle of sparkling wine.)

              JANELLE
I love this honey. Thanks very much.

              KEVIN
Your welcome, baby.

(Janelle and Kevin kiss, toast, and eat their
meal.)

ACT THREE SCENE SEVEN Janelle's patio May 2009.

> (Janelle's sitting on her front porch reading the 25th *May* Edition of *"Ebony"* magazine. As Janelle sips her cup of lemonade, her cell phone goes off.)

> (Janelle glances down at her phone.)

(Janelle sees Anthony's number flash across her cell phone.

>   JANELLE
It's Anthony calling me. I am beginning to feel knots almost the size of grape fruits in my stomach.

(Janelle sighs and shuts her eyes for a moment.)

>   JANELLE
Oh what's happening, it's as though I am reliving those moments. I remember clearly as if yesterday the numbness of my face and I visualize the black and blue marks around my eyes.

>   (Tears run down her face.)

(Janelle opens her teary eyes, looks up at the sky and sees a blackberry fall down from a Blackberry tree.)

(Janelle phone rings three times in a row.)

(She answers the phone.)

JANELLE

Hello.

ANTHONY

Hi Janelle, this is Anthony. How are you doing?

JANELLE

Great! I'm getting married. How are you?

ANTHONY

I've been better. I have Prostate cancer and I don't have much longer to live.

JANELLE

Really? I'm sorry Anthony. How did you get my number?

ANTHONY

Your Mom gave it to me.

(Janelle rolls her eyes.)

ANTHONY

It's alright. Hey I wanted to apologize to you for what I've done to you, Desera, Ebony, and Traci. I'm going to regret it for the rest of my life. I didn't realize what I had until I lost it.

                    JANELLE
I forgive you. Well, let me give you Desera's
number. You ready for the number?

                    ANTHONY
Yes.

                    JANELLE
It's . . .

                    ANTHONY
Thanks. How's Ebony and Traci.

                    JANELLE
They're both fine. You want to talk to them.

                    ANTHONY
Well, can you tell them hi for me?

                    JANELLE
I will. Take care.

ACT FOUR SCENE ONE Derek's apartment.

(Derek invites Desera over for dinner.
While Desera and Derek are enjoying their
candlelight dinner in Derek's blue and
white living room, Desera's cell phone
rings.)

(Desera answers her cell phone.)

DESERA
Hello?

ANTHONY
Hi Desera, it's your Dad, how are you doing?

(Desera pauses. She gently grabs Derek's right
hand.)

DESERA
Fine. How did you get my number?

ANTHONY
Your mom gave it to me.

DESERA
Okay. Why are you calling?

ANTHONY
I'm calling because I have Prostate cancer and
I don't have much longer to live.

DESERA
Sorry to hear that.

ANTHONY
I want to apologize to you.

DESERA
For?

ANTHONY
I wanted to apologize to you for what I've
done to you.

DESERA
Alright.

ANTHONY
So what are you doing tomorrow?

DESERA
Working. Why do you ask?

ANTHONY
I'll be in town tomorrow and I would like to
see you.

DESERA

        (She hesitates for a moment.)

Okay. I'll meet you outside of "*The New York
Star*" *around twelve noon*.

ANTHONY
See you then.

                DESERA
Bye.

                DEREK (hugs Desera.)
Are you alright boo?

                DESERA
Yeah, I'm nervous.

                DEREK
Baby, you don't have to be alone. I'll come
with you.

                DESERA
I'll be fine. Baby, I have to do this on my
own.

                DEREK
I love you.

                DESERA (Smiles.)
I love you too.

                DEREK
There's the smile I'm looking for.

ACT FOUR SCENE TWO Anthony's Visit April 2010.

> (Anthony is waiting outside "*The New York Star*" building. There's Blackberry and Maple trees everywhere.)

(As Desera strolls outside, her heart suddenly drops into her stomach.)

DESERA

Well, I see you made it.

> (Anthony sighs.)

ANTHONY

Yes, I did.

DESERA

So why did you come all of this way for?

ANTHONY

To see you.

DESERA

See me?

ANTHONY

Yes, I came here to see you.

DESERA

Why? I haven't seen you in five years, and if I'm not mistaken you left us, but I've forgiven you.

                    ANTHONY
I just wanted you to know how truly sorry I
am.

                    DESERA
Okay, I know.

                    DEREK
Well, I'm going to go now, but before I do, I
just want you to know that I'm proud of you.

                    DESERA
Alright, take care.

(Derek comes outside, sees Desera, and wraps
his arms around her.) .

                    DEREK
Hey.

                    DESERA
Hey.

                    DEREK
Is everything alright?

                    DESERA
Yeah, I'm fine. I'm happy because my father's
visit was necessary because it brought closer
to my life.

          (Derek kisses Desera.)

                    DEREK
Are you sure baby?

                    DESERA
Yes.

                    DEREK
Okay, just checking.

                    DESERA
You're sweet. I have to get back to work. I
need to finish my story.

(Maple leaves begin falling down on Desera and
Derek.)

ACT FOUR SCENE THREE The Restaurant
"Epiphany's" May 2010.

>(The restaurant is very eloquent and large. There are round tables with red satin table cloths and shiny silverware. On each table there's two tall red candles standing on *Hanging Glass Hurricane Tea Light* holders.)

>(As Derek pulls out the chair for Desera, a man with a violin comes in the room.)

>(The Violist is playing a song entitled *"Spend My Life with You,"* by *Eric Beret* and *Tamia*.)

(Desera's wearing a blue grown and Derek's wearing a light blue dress shirt and black slacks.)

>(Derek's palms are perspiring with sweat and his heart's beating rapidly.)

(Derek gently takes Desera's left hand, glazes into her brown eyes, and bends down on one knee.)

>(Desera smiles.)

>DESERA

Oh my God!

(Derek's heart is beating fast like a drum.)

(Desera sighs.)

(Derek's hands are shaking and his stomach is filled with various butterflies.)

             DEREK
Desera Harrison, I love you and I think the world of you. The first day that I laid eyes on you I thought you were amazing, smart, and sexy. You are a strong black woman who had to be your family's shield, strong tower, and rock. Well, I want to be your strong tower, and your night and shinny armor. I want to be the one that you can count on and trust. So I have a question for you.

             (Desera smiles.)

             DESERA
Yes.

             DEREK
Will you marry me?

             DESERA
Yes! Yes! I'll marry you!

             (Derek hugs Desera.)

             (Desera kisses Derek.)

             (Derek swings Desera around in circles.)

DEREK

Well, let's make a toast.

(Derek summons the waiter.)

THE WAITER

Can I get you something?

DEREK

Yes, can we get a bottle of Grey Goose please?

THE WAITER

Coming right up.

ACT FOUR SCENE FOUR Janelle's wedding. Summer 2010.

> (It's mid June and it's Janelle and Kevin's wedding. It couldn't be a more perfect day; the sky is clear and blue. The sun is shining through the Baptist church.)

(The church is large and has red and white satin flower petals on the edges of the eight foot red carpet.)

> (The church is filled to capacity.)

(As the wedding song begins, the church congregation rises, and the back doors slowly opens.)

(Janelle is escorted down the aisle by her father.)

My Inspiration

Lyrics

(Four bars of melodic harmonizing flowing throughout the Church)

You have a positive

Spirit . . . Spirit

(Harmonizing) that brightens

My gloomy days . . . My gloomy days

My inspiration

The one who

Has given me

Love and accepts

All my flaws . . .

My inspiration
(My inspiration)
My joy, my love,
My everything . . . Everything . . .

Your strong believe
In Jesus is so
Amazing like a
Artist painting
A scenery of a
Majestic waterfall

You're so amazing
(Amazing)
A heartfelt man
Who inspires and
Encourages . . . Encourages . . .
Encourages . . . Me . . . . You're my inspiration

You're my breakfast
In the morning that
Lifts me up
As a motivated speech
You are my protector
The one who . . . Loves . . . . me . . . .
(Jovial Smith)

(Reverend Charles walks up to the pulpit.)

REVEREND CHARLES
We are gathered together to witness this couple
in marriage.

(Janelle and Kevin face each other.)

REVEREND CHARLES
Janelle repeat after me.

(Janelle repeats)

I, Janelle Harrison, take Kevin Jones to be my husband, to have and to hold you from this day forward, for better or for worse, for richer, or for poorer, in sickness and in health. I, further promise to love you and cherish you, and be faithful to you for as long as we both shall live.

REVEREND CHARLES
Kevin, repeat after me.

(KEVIN repeats)

I, Kevin Jones take Janelle Harrison, to be my wife, to have and to hold you from this day forward, for better or for worse, for richer, or for poorer, in sickness and in health. I further promise to love you and cherish you, and be faithful to you for as long as we both shall live.

REVEREND CHARLES
By the power invested in me I now pronounce you husband and wife. You may kiss your bride.

(Kevin kisses Janelle.)

(Ebony and Traci hug Janelle and Kevin.)

EBONY
I'm happy for you both.

TRACI
I'm happy for you two.

(Desera and Derek hug Janelle and Kevin.)

DESERA
I'm happy too. Mom, I'm so happy for you because you've been through so much. I'm proud of you Mommy. You've overcame the physical abuse that we endured by our father. Most of all, for taking care of Ebony, Traci, and myself.

JANELLE (eyes tearing up)
Thanks baby. I'm proud of you to for becoming a beautiful and strong woman who has found the strength to overcome the physical abuse.

(Then Desera turns to hug Derek.)

DESERA
Kevin make sure that you take good care of my mom okay.

KEVIN
I will.

DESERA(Desera smiles.)
I'm sure you will.

DEREK

Well baby in a year and some change it will be
you and I.

(Desera kisses Derek.)

DESERA

I can't wait.

KEVIN

I can't wait either.

ACT FOUR SCENE FIVE Derek's and Desera's engagement party Fall 2010.

> (Desera and Derek have invited their family and friends over for cocktails and finger foods.) (Everyone's gathered in the living room chatting and catching up with one another.)

> (Love and laughter filled the room.)

(There's R&B music playing in the background.)

(Desera taps her wine glass to get everyone's attention.)

> (The room goes silent.)

DESERA

First of all, Derek and I want to thank each and every one of you for coming. You being here, means a lot to us. I feel the love in this room. Would you like to say something babe?

DEREK

Thanks for coming. I'm happy and I'm looking forward in spending the rest of my life with this beautiful black queen.

> (Desera smiles.)

> (Derek kisses Desera.)

(Janelle stands up and speaks.)

JANELLE

Well Desera, I'm very proud of the strong woman that you have become. Sometimes I don't understand why God allows situations to happen in our lives' but all I know is that it has made you stronger.

(Desera hugs Janelle.)

(Desera takes a seat.)

Janelle

Your sister Ebony has something to show you.

EBONY

Hey sis, I want to read you my poem about you.

(Ebony shares her poem entitled "*A Picture of a woman.*")

EBONY (reads)
A Picture of a Woman

A woman who shows confidence is like a person
Who won a brand new car and shows pride
Pride that expresses radiance throughout the room
People who are attracted to this type of
woman see her as . . .
A rose that is fully bloomed

A woman shows compassion for other people
Compassion that is sincere like
A man proposing to his future fiancé
A mother getting her child a favorite gift
A mother who gazes into her newborn child's
eyes
Thanking God for the gift that she has

A woman who is independent
Obtains a radiant glow
Her presence calms an unsettling spirit
Nurtures the heart with her angelic voice
She is very boastful but humble
Like a seed that is slowly unfolding into an
eloquent sunflower

A woman's vulnerability is as delicate as a
sunflower
Strong, loving, and caring
A strong woman obtains authority that is
Powerful as a lion.

(Desera strolls up to Ebony and hugs her.)

DESERA
Thanks sweetie.

TRACI (she smiles.)
Well Desera, I painted a picture of you and
Derek. In the background I painted two trees,
a Blackberry and a Maple tree. These trees
represent perseverance and strength.

111

                    DESERA
Thanks Ebony and Traci, I love you both and
thanks again for your gifts.

                    DESERA AND DEREK
Thanks for coming tonight. We love everyone.

ACT FIVE SCENE ONE "The New York Star" Headquarters."

(Desera is sitting at her desk typing away.)

DESERA

I am extremely busy writing responses to many women who have expressed their thoughts and feelings on domestic violence. One writer who really stands out is an eighteen year old teenage girl named Regina Knowles because her story is almost identical to mine.

(Desera sips her coffee.)

(She glances through various stories that are related to hers, Desera comes across the name *Regina Knowles.*

(Desera reads Regina letter.)

DESERA

Dear Desera,
Reading your story has really broken the silence of domestic violence for many women like myself. When you're in a family that seems to appear normal and happy on the outside, but behind closed doors all hell breaks loose, you can feel trapped. The screams and sounds can be very intense like someone who's begging for his or her life. You're life is not being taking form you in a physical sense, but in a psychological sense. The way that one can break free from this nightmare is to break

the silence by expressing yourself verbally.
Thank you and hopefully I will get a chance to
meet you soon.

Signed Sincerely, Regina Knowles.)

    (Desera sighs.)

    (Derek knocks on the door.)

        DEREK
Hey babe, are you busy?

        DESERA (Smiles)
I'm never too busy for you.

        DEREK
Well I have someone who's excited to meet
you.

        DESERA
Alright, bring them in.

(Regina walks in and Desera rises from her
chair.)

        REGINA
Hi, I'm Regina, nice to meet you.

        DESERA
Same here. First of all, I want to say that I
was touched by your story because I saw you

overcoming struggles and insecurities such as
I once had at one point in time.

(As Desera and Regina are chatting, Desera
glances at the window. She's intrigued by the
scenery.)

(As the Maple and Blackberry leaves come down
like a rain shower, Desera glances down and
sees her family and glances over at Regina.)

DESERA
Regina, do you mind if we take this conversation
outside?

REGINA
No I don't mind.

(Desera and Regina rushes out of the office to
join Desera's family.)

(Desera thinks out loud to herself.)

DESERA
*Looking back on life, meaning where I've been
and how far my family have come, makes me
humble. I have realized that everyone who has
breath in their body will have times where
they laugh and nights where they sit on the
edge of their bed crying. Standing here with
my family laughing and enjoying their company
makes me content. Seeing the smiles on my mom,
Ebony, and Traci's face makes me feel like*

everything that we have been through was not in vein. You see, I may not have had a perfect childhood, but by the grace of God, I was able to be strong and to persevere no matter what life brings. So I believe that Blackberry Molasses means, if everyone who struggles with situations that may seem unbearable, just keep in mind that trouble is only for a season, and God will make a way for him or her. For tomorrow is one day closer to your way out; a step closer to your goals and dreams that you're striving to reach.)

-THE END-

About the Author

Jovial (Joy) Nicole Smith *was born on Friday May 6, 1983 in Inglewood California. Jovial believes strongly in the Lord and Savior Jesus Christ and keeps Him close to her heart. This strong woman may have a disability known as Cerebral Palsy, but she doesn't let this minor setback stop her from reaching and achieving her goals. In fact, when people would tell Jovial things such as "You will never go to college because it's too difficult!" . . ."Your dad is not going to let you live on your own!" . . . "Joy, you shouldn't set yourself*

*up for failure!" . . . and the list goes on...
it gave her more incentive to reach her goals.
Despite all the negativity, Jovial was able
to achieve everything people said that she
wouldn't be able to do!!!*

   *During Jovial's educational experience,
she attended C.T. Reed Elementary, Eisenhower
Middle, and Laurel High school. Jovial attended
St. Andrews Presbyterian college where she
received her Bachelor's Degree in Creative
Writing with a Minor in English. She also
attended East Carolina University where she
received her Master's in English Literature.
This gifted writer is an author of two poetry
books entitled "Angelic Voices" 'and "Defining
Moments." This remarkable woman has also
written five other poetry books entitled "A
Woman Destined For Success," "A Blessing in
Disguise," "Expressions of The Heart," "Love
Chronicles," and "The Essence Of A Poets Heart."
Jovial's play entitled "Blackberry Molasses"
is her current publication. This talented woman
is a passionate poet that birth out words
filled with hope, compassion, perseverance,
diligence, and faith. She's a voice for those
who are often looked down upon because he or
she is different. This gifted woman is also a
Play-writer, a Songwriter, a Creative writer,
who floods the minds of others with inspiring
words; motivating and encouraging them to
discover their gifts and talents." Jovial
believes that "inspiration comes from within.
Searching for your dreams may be tiring but*

as you keep persevering you will reach your dreams and have much success."

-Jovial Smith-

Jovial Smith

NOTES

NOTES

NOTES

NOTES